DK ESSENTIAL MANAGERS

Leadership

CHRISTINA OSBORNE

D0981057

London, New York, Melbourne, Munich, and Delhi

Senior Editor Peter Jones
Senior Art Editor Helen Spencer
Executive Managing Editor Adèle Hayward
Managing Art Editor Kat Mead
Art Director Peter Luff
Publisher Stephanie Jackson
Production Editor Ben Marcus
Production Controller Hema Gohil
US Editor Charles Wills

Produced for Dorling Kindersley Limited by

cobaltid

The Stables, Wood Farm, Deopham Road,
Attleborough, Norfolk NR17 1AJ
www.cobaltid.co.uk

Editors Louise Abbott, Kati Dye, Maddy King,
Marek Walisiewicz
Designers Darren Bland, Claire Dale, Paul Reid,
Annika Skoog, Lloyd Tilbury, Shane Whiting

First American Edition, 2008

Published in the United States by DK Publishing
375 Hudson Street, New York, New York 10014

10 11   10 9 8 7 6 5 4 3 2 1

DD471—September 2008

Published in Great Britain by
Dorling Kindersley Limited.

A catalog record for this book is available from
the Library of Congress.

ISBN 978-0-7566-3705-7

DK books are available at special discounts
when purchased in bulk for sales promotions,
premiums, fund-raising, or educational use.
For details, contact: DK Publishing Special Markets,
375 Hudson Street, New York, New York 10014 or
SpecialSales@dk.com.

Color reproduction
by Colourscan, Singapore
Printed in China by Starlite

Discover more at **www.dk.com**

Contents

Introduction

Leadership is the ability to create an environment where everyone knows what contribution is expected and feels totally committed to doing a great job. Leadership is an essential skill for all successful managers to learn and practice regularly.

This book explains the key techniques leaders use to release their own and their team's full potential. It shows you how to think and take action with a leadership approach and to look at yourself and the world around you with a leadership focus.

Practical advice is given to help you to develop the leadership aspects of your own role and to encourage leadership and initiative from everyone in your team. From taking up a leadership role to leading with confidence in difficult situations, this book prepares you step-by-step for all the challenges leaders face.

The book is packed with advice to help you direct your energy toward building essential relationships and achieving the most important results that add value to your organization and identify you as a successful leader of people.

Chapter 1

Understanding leadership

When you take up a leadership role, you will be expected to tackle multiple tasks—from meeting goals through to developing new opportunities—while making sure your team follows you and your organization's vision and values.

Defining the challenge

If you thrive on thinking creatively, inspiring and guiding people, experimenting with different approaches, and making intuitive decisions, you are on the way to being a leader. However, truly accomplished leaders also possess sound analytical and problem-solving skills.

Thinking leadership

*Life principle—
a rule, belief, or
moral code that is
important to you
and guides your
decision-making
throughout life.

Leaders are made rather than born. And while a real desire to lead is a prerequisite for leadership, the skills you need to lead can be learned. Leadership has many facets and no simple definition: it is the ability to inspire and encourage others to overcome challenges, accept continuous change, and achieve goals; it is the capacity to build strong, effective teams; and it is the process of using your influence to persuade and steer. Leaders set a strong example through their own life principles*; they achieve results but also take responsibility for failure.

Leading and managing

Leadership is different from management. A leader is someone who makes decisions and communicates bold messages, while a manager implements strategies, measures performance, and runs systems. You probably aspire to be called a leader rather than a manager. Being a leader is exciting; being a manager is mundane. Of course, like most stereotypes, the statements above contain a measure of truth, but sound management requires some leadership, and great leaders are—or at least know what it takes to be—good managers.

When you move into a leadership role you won't and can't abandon managing altogether; to be credible as leader, you need to acknowledge the past and what is currently happening, at the same time as focusing on the future.

BEING A LEADER

FAST TRACK	**OFF TRACK**
Learning quickly what motivates team members	Thinking yesterday's result will still count tomorrow
Asking your team for their view on the situation	Being out of touch with your own emotions
Thinking beyond what happens now	Not noticing what is going on around you
Knowing how to train and develop your team	Not asking for feedback on your leadership and ideas
Setting standards to build a team you can rely on	Not keeping physically fit and thinking positively

TIP

BE AGILE
To be a good leader, stay close to your team, and use your judgement to move between leadership and management roles as necessary.

Leading from within

The job of a leader is to gift others a sense of purpose and self-worth. This is impossible to do with any conviction if you don't understand your own strengths and weaknesses, or if you are uncertain about the direction in which you want to take your professional and personal life. Improving self-awareness is an essential part of growing into a more effective leader and becoming alert to the effects you are having on others.

TIP

LIST YOUR SKILLS
Make a list of the characteristics you already have as a leader—"I am focused", "I am committed to excellence", "I respect others", "I work hard"—and those to which you aspire: "I am caring", "I am trusted". Repeat this exercise often to monitor your inner development.

Being a frontrunner

People respect leaders who embrace strong values and take responsibility for their own choices in life. To demonstrate this internal strength you need to be seen to be leading by example. Show your team that you have the confidence to take risks, that you can persist through difficult times, and that you are prepared to keep on learning, adapting, and creating new business opportunities.

Developing self-awareness

To be effective, you need to lead from the inside out. What you really think, and what you value as your life principles, should emerge clearly in your behavior. To think as a leader, you should look to your self-awareness as well as to your awareness of the outside world. Leading from within is not just about being true to your own principles: it also brings results. When you embrace the values by which you live and apply them to your role as a leader, people will respect your sincerity, acknowledge the stake you have in your work and in your team, and sense that you wish others to succeed. Self-awareness means analyzing your thoughts and emotions, seeking as much feedback from others as possible, and developing listening skills.

Knowing yourself

People don't all think in the same way. Understanding your own thinking style and the styles of others around you will give you some valuable leadership tools. The term "thinking style" does not refer to your IQ, but how you process information; broadly we can distinguish between three styles: tactical, operational, and strategic.

Most people tend to get stuck using just one of the thinking styles. But by recognizing your own thinking style you begin to ask different questions and think about problems in fresh and exciting new ways. By doing this you work more effectively with your team because you can understand how they think and communicate, and you can talk to people in their own "language."

DEFINING THINKING STYLES

STYLE	CHARACTERISTICS	QUESTIONS ASKED
Tactical	• Accepts direction • Focuses on how to achieve a goal • Plans and thinks through any actions logically	• How can we achieve the best result in the least time? • How can we organize the actions into a clear plan? • What are the most important things to do or coordinate?
Operational	• Sees opportunities for action and improvement • Focuses on practical actions and implementation in complex situations	• What action can we take? • What needs to be done? • When can we start?
Strategic	• Thinks any problems out from first principles • Redefines problems and confidently challenges upward	• What if...? • Why have we ruled out these other courses of action? • Why not do this instead? • Who else needs to be involved?

Applying self-knowledge

The benefits of self-knowledge in the workplace may not be immediately apparent when set alongside other, more practical and cognitive skills, but its value has been acknowledged by psychologists for decades. The term Emotional Intelligence (EI) was coined to describe an ability to identify, discriminate between, and use one's own and others' feelings to guide your thoughts and actions. The importance of EI cannot be overstated—there are many studies that indicate that EI is a far better indicator of leadership potential than standard measures of intelligence such as IQ. The emotions that leaders experience affect the culture of an organization, shaping employee satisfaction, loyalty, and productivity, and so having a real influence on results.

TIP

COMMIT TO CHANGE

Seek out an experienced coach to guide you in building EI. The transformation means you changing your attitudes and habits, as well as learning new skills, and requires a real commitment—in time and resources—from you and from your organization.

Assessing the benefits

At a basic level, it is easy to see that understanding and controlling your inner self has some real applications that benefit you and the organization:
• Being able to control your temper, to elevate yourself from boredom, or to turn dejection into positive energy are all desirable abilities.
• Recognizing that sad or negative moods tend to bring your focus on to details, while happy moods direct you to new ideas and solutions, improves your productivity, and helps time management.
• Confronting and analyzing your fears may illuminate a problem you are facing, so saving time.
Expertise in the key competencies of EI opens the door to more sophisticated ways of forming and sustaining productive relationships. What's more, these competencies can be learned through training and practice so you can change your behavior in a genuine, sustained manner.

Using Emotional Intelligence

RECOGNIZING EMOTIONS
• Accurately identifying and categorizing your own feelings and the feelings of others.
• Being aware, moment-by-moment, of what you are feeling.

REGULATING EMOTIONS
• Recognizing that how you feel influences how you think.
• Knowing which of your moods are best for different situations.
• Not letting others manipulate your emotions.

USING EMOTIONS
• Using deliberate strategies to make your feelings—even negative ones—work for you.
• Harnessing emotions so that you can take positive actions, even in the face of difficulty.

EMPATHIZING
• Recognizing that emotions provide information about others.
• Being able to see a situation from another's point-of-view.

NURTURING
• Genuinely caring for others.
• Showing real appreciation for peoples' contributions.
• Having others' best interests at heart when setting goals.

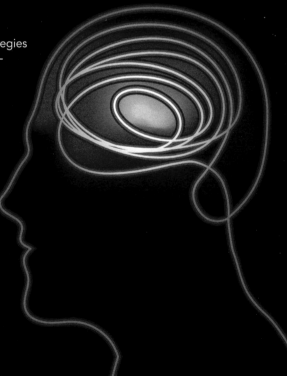

Leading through vision

As a business leader, you will be expected to set out the values of an organization and provide its stakeholders with an emotionally appealing and achievable vision* of the future. Clear, thoughtful communication at every level is needed in order to develop this vision and translate it into medium-term strategies and day-to-day action.

Setting out the vision

EXPLAIN WHY

"Why" needs to be explained in two ways: "Because of A…" (referring to a past/present reason) and "In order to do B…" (explaining future consequences).

Leaders focus on vision and overall aims and then help their team members to interpret how to achieve the agreed objectives in a way consistent with the organization's values. Your leadership role may be to create the vision and strategic objectives at the top of your organization, or it may be to develop your team plan in alignment with a bigger corporate strategy.

In either case, the best way to move forward is to involve your team in developing the vision right from the start. Begin by writing it down. As you move forward, you will need to restate and recreate the vision through open question and answer sessions, team meetings, and one-to-one reviews. Soon each person will learn how to make a meaningful individual contribution toward team goals.

People are motivated by a clear understanding of what they need to do to fulfil the vision, by when, how well, and why. These are key signposts on the journey to their professional development and to the achievement of the team's vision. Your job is to help everyone in your team to plan the route, and to review their progress.

*vision—*a word picture of your future as an organization or team. It describes what things will look like when we get to where we want to be.*

Working with teams

Your key role as leader is to inspire emotional attachment to an attractive vision and to make success visible. People will then believe in cause and effect—that individual performance counts and doing their best really does lead to a better life for all concerned.

• **Give everyone a role** to play in implementing the team vision and ask them to report back to you on what has gone exceptionally well and what not so well.
• **Ask individuals** to present highlights to the rest of the team so that everyone can learn about doing things in new ways. When you review these practical steps with the team, keep linking them back to the overall vision.
• **Remember to say** "thank you" individually and in front of the team to help them keep their momentum and motivation.

Q IN FOCUS...
JUST REWARDS

Think laterally about the way you reward members of your team. Financial rewards often have less motivational value than your recognition and thanks. If you are respected by your team, your greatest gift is your time. Schedule time to give full attention to each person in your team at regular intervals. Never over-promise and under-deliver future benefits to your team members.

• **Celebrate team successes** to keep the team moving forward together. Recognize even small steps in the right direction.
• **Explore** with individual team members their unique mix of values, life experiences, knowledge, and skills plus potential abilities. Understand what specifically motivates each person to engage with their work and willingly release the extra they have to give.

Growing with your role

Growth is built in to the vision of most organizations; and when an organization grows, its leaders must be prepared to adapt with it. Your role as a leader may become bigger and more strategic with each organizational transition, so anticipating change is a cornerstone of thinking like an effective leader.

Start-up

When an organization starts up, it is entrepreneurial—focused on delivering a new service to new customers. Communication is informal, and people are prepared to put in long hours. Customer feedback is quick and the small group of people responds rapidly with enthusiasm and energy.

Leadership at this stage is about keeping close to customers and staff, and encouraging new ideas. As a leader, you may well be involved in frontline activities.

Rapid growth

As the organization grows, you may start to see problems with the quality of delivery. Communication with the team may become more formal and some of the initial energy and initiative can be lost. More of your time will be spent on designing and implementing systems, structures, and standards.

At this stage, you need to work hard at remaining accessible to people who seek your advice and resist retreating into a purely management role.

Continued growth

The next organizational transition occurs when you begin to realize that you can no longer control everything—there are simply not enough hours in the day. You may notice that team members are complaining about how long it takes for decisions to be made. They may ask for greater freedom to make their own decisions.

At this point, you should begin to recognize the need to delegate—essential if you are to retain and develop staff. You should put more of your time and effort into leadership and communication and less into your original expertise—for example, accounting, sales, marketing, engineering, or operations.

Devolution

As the organization continues to grow, you may be part of a core leadership team directing strategy and coordination, while a group of managers in business units lead teams on a devolved basis.

You need to become a strong communicator because a significant part of your role is resolving tensions between devolved units and the center. You need to manage relationships to ensure that all parts of the organization work collaboratively and are fully committed to the overall strategy. Bear in mind the development of future leaders is essential to the long-term survival of the organization and is another one of your new responsibilities.

Chapter 2

Taking up your leadership role

When you are given a leadership position, you need to prepare yourself for intense learning and adaptation. From getting your feet under the desk to developing your competences, there are many challenges in store.

Preparing to lead

When you become a leader, you need to quickly understand what is expected from you and from your team. Your employer will provide you with guidance, but don't assume that you'll get the complete picture. A lot of the groundwork is going to be up to you.

Giving yourself a headstart

It pays to prepare for your leadership role even before your first day on the job. Do some basic groundwork and research: ask your employer where you fit into their organizational plans; ask when you will be expected to produce objectives for your team; and when and how your performance—and that of your team—will be assessed. Talk to the outgoing leader about the demands of the role and the team dynamics. Research your team: request performance figures and personnel files; ask the outgoing leader and your peers what information will be of most use.

Managing data

Throughout the first few weeks in your new role, you will be deluged with information. Unfortunately, you won't necessarily know which of this data is of strategic importance, and which is just minor detail. Head off early errors by being systematic; file the information and make a list of what you have received. Review this list weekly and try to place the relative significance of each piece of information in a broader context.

You'll also be introduced to many new people. Always carry a notebook and pencil with you; after each meeting, make a note of the name, position, and distinguishing features of the person you have met, along with anything memorable they said to you. When you meet them next, you'll remember who they are and how they fit into the organization. What's more, you'll be able to pick up your conversation with them.

Being realistic

Your arrival as a team's new leader will raise expectations of change for the better. However, you may discover that some expectations are less than realistic. For example, your team's previous leader may have provided detailed guidance on how work should be carried out; if your leadership style is more about empowering your team to make their own decisions, they may initially feel poorly supported and even resentful of the added responsibility. Early in your tenure, ask others what assumptions they have about you and your role.
• Outline what success looks like to you. Does their view match yours?
• What expectations do they have of how long things will take?
• Have they been made any unrealistic promises about what you will deliver?
You can then begin to address any discrepancies between their expectations and your reality.

 CHECKLIST EXCHANGING INFORMATION

	YES	NO
• Have you had or requested an induction briefing?	☐	☐
• Have you identified areas in your new role where you need training?	☐	☐
• Have you studied the company's organization charts?	☐	☐
• If you have been promoted, have you told your existing contacts in the organization of your new role?	☐	☐
• Do you know which meetings you are expected to attend?	☐	☐

Focusing your energy

As a leader, you are likely to be inundated with communications, requests, new tasks, and initiatives. Recognizing—and focusing on— what is really important is critical to your success and that of your team; it is vital that how you spend your time reflects your priorities.

TIP

MAKE ROOM FOR CONTINGENCIES
You should set aside time with your team to brainstorm likely barriers to delivering on time. Reserve at least 10 percent of overall project time for contingencies.

Managing your time

It is easy to get distracted from key tasks by less important, but nonetheless urgent activities. Prioritizing your actions is something you should schedule in every day, and approach with discipline. A simple solution is to write a "to do" list at the end of each day. Scrutinize this list, assessing each item against your vision, values, and key objectives; then, number each item in order of priority. Alternatively, try categorizing your tasks more systematically under the four headings shown opposite.

WORKING SMART

FAST TRACK	**OFF TRACK**
Improving standards	Doing work you could delegate
Building networks	Never leaving your office
Recording and analyzing how you spend your time	Reacting to stimuli as they arrive
Being realistic about durations	Starting without a clear schedule

HOW TO PRIORITIZE TASKS

HIGH URGENCY
LOW IMPORTANCE

Typical activities
- Dealing with phone calls and emails as they come in
- Dealing with others' priorities not in line with your vision

What happens when you spend time on this
- Lack of clear goals
- Crisis management
- Feeling out of control
- Behaving inconsistently

Action Delegate it

HIGH URGENCY
HIGH IMPORTANCE

Typical activities
- Dealing with crises
- Being closely involved with time-critical projects
- Attending key meetings

What happens when you spend time on this
- Constant crisis management
- Exhaustion and stress
- Burnout over the long-term

Action Do it now, but review your time planning

LOW URGENCY
LOW IMPORTANCE

Typical activities
- Low-level meetings
- Timewasting
- Unfocused browsing

What happens when you spend time on this
- Failure to take responsibility
- Inability to complete jobs
- Increased dependence on others
- Insecurity

Action Leave it

LOW URGENCY
HIGH IMPORTANCE

Typical activities
- Planning ahead
- Anticipating problems
- Guiding and training the team
- Delegating
- Building relationships

What happens when you spend time on this
- Overview
- Vision
- Balance

Action Schedule it

Getting back on track

Missed or delayed deadlines and recurring problems that you never seem to get around to fixing are symptoms of faulty time management. If the root cause is not addressed, your work life could soon run out of control, sapping your energy and stifling your creativity. Stop, take some time out, and refocus your thoughts. Plan in some time to address strategic activities, and think what and how you could improve delegation within your team.

TIP

**CARRY OUT
A DEBRIEF**

Once a task is complete, allow time for a debrief—discuss what went well, and what did not. How would you change the process next time? What was learned? Was this a suitable task to delegate to the individual?

Delegating successfully

Delegation is a critical leadership skill, and one that—when done well—has great benefits for you and your team. It liberates your schedule, makes members of your team feel valued, and develops capabilities throughout the organization. Delegating well requires more than just handing a task over to a subordinate:

• Choose carefully who you delegate a task to. Assess the probability of things going wrong.

• Only delegate tasks that can be clearly defined. If you can't specify the desired outcome and timeframe, it is unreasonable to expect someone to succeed.

• Delegate time-consuming, recurring tasks.

• Establish and agree milestones, working procedures, resources, and deadlines.

• Check that the person to who you are delegating shares your understanding of the task in hand.

• Monitor progress and provide support—you cannot abdicate responsibility after delegating.

• Delegating means allowing people to find their own solutions: you must accept that these will not necessarily be the same as your solutions.

• Don't apportion blame if things don't work out: remember it is you who shoulders responsibility for ultimate success or failure.

Selecting personnel

To identify the best member of your team to take on a particular task, try using a "Plan to Delegate" table, such as the sample below, to give a degree of objectivity. To use the Plan to Delegate table:
• List all members of your team.
• Devise your criteria for choosing someone—those on the sample table are a good starting point.
• Rate each member of your team for all criteria from 1–10.

• Add the scores.
• Add comments on the amount and type of training, development, or support each individual needs.

When you carry out this exercise, the best fit candidate is not always the most obvious. You may have developed the habit of just asking one experienced and skilled team member to do jobs for you. However, others on the team may have more time to devote to the task, and will benefit from the experience and responsibility.

PLAN TO DELEGATE

CRITERIA	JANE	JIM	JOHN
Current capability and experience	8	7	4
Skills/competences	7	8	5
Development potential	9	7	9
Availability	3	9	9
Motivation/commitment	8	4	9
Task consistent with individual's goals for development	5	3	7
Total score	40	38	43
Other comments, such as training or support needed	None	Needs constant motivation	Needs training on template usage
Milestones/reviews	Review at end of task	Review frequently	Review at first milestone and end only

Working at relationships

From your earliest days as a leader, you will need to build relationships with your team and a range of stakeholders throughout the organization. The ability to understand and influence people is a key skill, and thinking of relationships in terms of "stories" gives you some tools to analyze and control your interactions.

LISTEN TO THE SUBTEXT

Listen for recurrent patterns in peoples' stories. What do they tell you about the way they relate to others, their modes of thinking, biases, and barriers?

Telling stories

We each carry in our heads our own stories—the narratives we have constructed over the years to make sense of our collected experiences, emotions, habits, and thoughts. These stories bias our perspective in all new situations and may push us toward embracing the future or—conversely—constrain our actions.

Relationships are built by exchanging these stories with other people—disclosing more of ourselves, our backgrounds, roles, and beliefs—and creating new, emergent stories. Just as individuals have their own stories, so do organizations; these stories encompass the history and values of that organization and describe how they get things done.

Listening to stories

By listening analytically to a person's story, you may be able to understand why they want to work with you and what their motivations are likely to be. Stories point to ways of negotiating successfully with individuals or companies, and even indicate whether a joint venture is likely to succeed. Leaders who fail to take account of a person's or an organization's past thoughts, culture, actions, and aspirations—as well as what they observe in the present—can find themselves facing an unexpected culture clash.

Learning about people through their stories

Do the stories place the individual in a particular role—hero, participant, or victim, for example?

Are the stories explorative and adventurous, or conservative, focused on maintaining equilibrium?

Do the stories convey a strong moral code, judgments, or beliefs?

Do the stories make or break connections between things?

Are the stories mostly set in the past, present, or future?

Do the stories express themselves in protective jargon?

Do the stories claim particular skills for the individual?

TIP

KEEP TALKING

Keep dialog open with all stake-holders. Sound relationships—and new stories—are built layer by layer through a series of conversations that ask questions as well as offering answers.

Learning from stories

By listening to the stories told by people—and by organizations—you can gain an insight into what types of relationships they will tend to form.

By understanding the very nature of the relationship, you will be able to modify your own behavior to best advantage. Most people—and indeed organizations—tend to fit into one of four main categories of relationship-building:

• **I win, you lose** This person has a need to control or compete. Their main reason for wanting a relationship with you is to achieve their own goals. Their concern is primarily for their own interests and they will bargain you down so that they achieve more.

• **I lose, you win** This person needs to belong and will prioritize the relationship above their own interests. They will always try to accommodate your wishes if you state them clearly and offer goodwill gestures.

• **I lose, you lose** This person has a strong desire to avoid conflict—indeed this is their primary concern in any relationship. They may focus on trivial issues to avoid areas of potential disagreement.

• **I win, you win** This person wants to collaborate. He or she is concerned for both parties' needs and wants to reach consensus or use lateral thinking to explore a better solution so that everyone wins. Leaders and organizations like this are good at building new narratives about new possibilities.

CASE STUDY

Merging cultures

A merger between a large international company (A) and a smaller, but dynamic national company (B) was jeopardized when rumors emerged that the merger would be accompanied by redundancies in B. The directors of both companies failed to conduct an open exchange of company stories, and did not discuss how both cultures would align to a new story after the merger. Planned communication was replaced by stories exchanged informally on the grapevine, which were overly pessimistic.

Pinpointing key relationships

You cannot hope to forge a strong relationship with everyone in your organization. As a leader, you need to concentrate your efforts on key stakeholders—those people who have the biggest investment in a project, or whose influence can help or hinder progress. To identify key stakeholders, start by asking yourself and your team who will gain or lose the most from your actions, and who is in a position to affect success. Be sure to consider internal and external parties, including suppliers, customers, directors, and in-house departments. Next, plot all the stakeholders on to a chart, similar to that below, so you can more clearly assess the importance and type of relationship you should establish with each type of stakeholder.

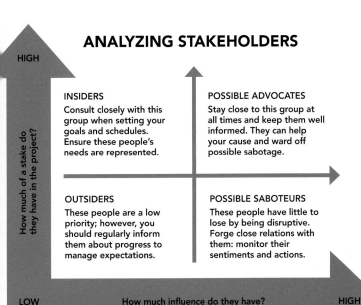

ANALYZING STAKEHOLDERS

HIGH

How much of a stake do they have in the project?

INSIDERS
Consult closely with this group when setting your goals and schedules. Ensure these people's needs are represented.

POSSIBLE ADVOCATES
Stay close to this group at all times and keep them well informed. They can help your cause and ward off possible sabotage.

OUTSIDERS
These people are a low priority; however, you should regularly inform them about progress to manage expectations.

POSSIBLE SABOTEURS
These people have little to lose by being disruptive. Forge close relations with them: monitor their sentiments and actions.

LOW   How much influence do they have?   HIGH

Using competences

How can you define what you need to become an effective leader? You may get some inspiration from the lives of great business, political, and military leaders of the past. However, a more reliable way of shaping your objectives is to use competences—descriptions of performance outputs that characterize leadership in your organization.

Emulating the greats

Bookshops are lined with the biographies of famous leaders, which tell us how they acted and dealt with adversity. A lesson that emerges from their life stories is that you lead from who you are. To lead effectively, you must be comfortable in your own skin and live a life according to your own principles. So much as you admire Ghandi or Che Guevara, you can't copy them—this will give rise to inconsistent behaviors that will be interpreted as indecisiveness or insincerity.

Setting objective targets

A more realistic way to shape your aims as a leader is through competences. These short describers set out the behaviors we would like to see in ourselves as leaders. Competences define what effective performance as a leader looks like and—through self-assessment and feedback—help leaders to identify their development needs. You can use a standard set of leadership competences to review your current performance and set objectives, or devise your own after carrying out suitable research and consultation.

STANDARD LEADERSHIP COMPETENCES

COMPETENCE	DESCRIPTION OF COMPETENCE
Achieving excellent results	• Delivers with energy and determination on individual, team, and overall objectives that address core business issues and contribute to achieving longer-term sustainable organizational goals • Behaves in a professional and ethical way
Building relationships	• Builds trust, listens to needs, is open to ideas, and sensitive to the perceptions of others • Questions constructively, identifies options and collaborates to develop solutions by networking and creating relationships with strategic people and organizations • Is able to work autonomously or in teams, adapt to a wide range of situations, and appreciate diversity • Remains aware of the needs and concerns of others and is consistently able to focus on objectives and build relationships, even when working under pressure or in the face of personal criticism in challenging situations • Good at selecting the right people with complementary strengths to work in teams
Coaching and communicating	• Communicates a clear vision of the organization's future • Enthuses and energizes people, is accessible to people, and gains ownership of the steps needed to achieve goals • Knows own and team members' strengths and weaknesses and encourages initiative, accountability for objectives, and the taking on of more responsibility • Invests time in coaching others and encourages effective contribution, gives constructive feedback, and knows when to support and challenge
Continuous innovation	• Experiments with new approaches • Learns from best practice, responds flexibly to change, and encourages others to question and review how things are done or could be continuously improved
Focusing on customers	• Achieves mutually beneficial relationships with customers • Manages expectations well in all interactions • Anticipates needs and responds with empathy
Lifetime learning and knowledge-sharing	• Keeps up-to-date, shares knowledge and information with other people, applies this learning to own work • Encourages others to learn, develop, and share knowledge
Solving problems and taking decisions	• Recognizes problems as opportunities, explores causes systematically and thoroughly • Generates ideas; weighs advantages and disadvantages of options

Writing your own competences

Using a set of standard competences—such as on the previous page—to define leadership roles may well be appropriate to you. Alternatively, you can identify and list competences by learning from others' experience—this is just one of the many benefits of joining a professional body for managers or leaders. The best option, however, would involve developing your own competences—ones that would accurately target your company's objectives and values.

Involving others

When writing competences for leaders, involve a cross-section of people in your organization. Start the discussion with the question, "What does being effective as a leader look like?" and invite people to contribute to the descriptions of the competences in terms that mean something to them. Combine the input from your staff with research on leadership best practice, and the knowledge you have about the future demands on leaders within the organization. Draft the competences with one eye always on their compatibility with the vision, values, and strategic objectives of the organization.

CASE STUDY

Putting competences to work

A leading professional institute wanted to define the behaviors of an effective leader. With involvement of the management team and a cross-section of staff from all departments, eight core leadership competences were identified and published in an internal document. A five-year leadership development program was designed to develop managers' competences. Development reviews, self-assessment, and feedback measured the progress of managers through a wide range of activities. The program included tailored workshops, case studies, action learning sets, executive coaching, and cross-functional projects that developed leadership and helped the organization to move forward its strategic plan.

Measuring and developing

After you have drafted the competences for a leadership role, you can begin to use them to develop your organization's leaders. The main vehicles for this are formal appraisals and self-assessment:

• Make sure the leader knows and fully understands what the competences are.

• Appoint a "competences advocate"—someone to encourage the leader to use the competences as a development tool.

• Agree the competences to be used in appraisals.

• Train appraisers throughout your organization in the meaning and use of competences.

• Encourage self-assessment against the benchmarks set by the competences.

When being assessed in an appraisal or carrying out self-assessment, it is helpful to recognize four stages of progress toward competence in a given area. So, for example, if you were to assess development in the competence "Solving problems and taking decisions," the results may be as shown below.

ASSESSING COMPETENCES: SOLVING PROBLEMS

STAGE OF DEVELOPMENT	ACTIONS DEMONSTRATED
Not yet demonstrated	Has only recently taken up the current role.
Developing	Finds it difficult to step back from the day-to-day operation and engage with others in creative problem-solving.
Competent	Encourages other people to put forward new ideas. Explores systematically to understand what is happening and why. Generates ideas to solve problems and decides on actions.
Role model/coach	Actively encourages others to think of problems and tensions as creative opportunities to improve service and develop products.

Providing feedback

The ability to both give and receive feedback is an essential leadership skill. Giving feedback encourages development and innovative thinking in your team, while knowing how to receive feedback provides an opportunity to learn more about yourself as a leader and the effect your behavior has on others.

TIP

LISTEN WELL
Be open in any feedback sessions. Other people will not approach everything in the same way as you, so listen to their suggestions.

Opening the dialogue

Giving feedback is not just about telling someone what you think. It is a two-way process that involves listening, asking questions, gaining commitment to change, summarizing what has been covered, and clarifying understanding. Feedback can be given informally in reviews or in quick one-to-one meetings.

Many organizations also provide appraisals—regular, formal opportunities for the exchange of feedback, which can include reviews of performance, development, or both. Appraisals happen at least annually and are usually between the line manager and team member although they can include others. Feedback from your boss, your team members, peers and customers is termed "360° feedback"; when segments are omitted (for example, feedback from customers and peers), the term is "180° feedback." Take time to prepare for a feedback session. Book a private room to ensure no interruptions. Always start positively, with the recipient's achievements: encourage them to talk about what has gone well. Avoid the tendency to focus more on mistakes they might have made than their strengths; make sure the positive feedback outweighs developmental points you bring up by at least 2:1.

Being specific and realistic

Feedback needs to be specific. Deal with one issue at a time rather than trying to tackle a number of issues at once. Be clear and direct in your comments: for example, "The way you gave the information and drew the diagram was really helpful to the customer", or "At that moment, I thought the customer felt uncomfortable because you seemed to be imposing your values, not just giving facts." General comments, such as "You were brilliant!" or "It was awful!" do not give the recipient any opportunities for learning.

Be realistic when using feedback—only refer to actions or behaviors that the person is able to change. You may have to start with small steps: for example, "It would help if you smiled more when you speak. I'm sure this would help our customers to feel really cared for." Gain agreement from each person on small goals, and praise people for having reached the standards you have previously defined.

Skilled feedback gives people information about their behavior and leaves them with a choice about how and if to act on it—change that is imposed too heavily will invite some degree of resistance.

Finally, always ask the recipient to summarize the actions they are going to take as a result of feedback—this helps you to double-check their understanding and commitment to change.

TIP

CONSIDER YOUR FEEDBACK
View a feedback session as a learning opportunity. Even if you are being critical, explain your point of view and give suggestions for improvement. Unskilled negative feedback will leave the recipient feeling negative and demotivated with nothing to build on except their feelings of resentment.

CHECKLIST
PREPARING TO GIVE FEEDBACK

	YES	NO
• Are you clear on what you want to say?	☐	☐
• Have you prepared a positive start and end to the feedback?	☐	☐
• Can you be specific in your developmental feedback?	☐	☐
• Is this the best time to give feedback?	☐	☐

Giving formal appraisals

When giving a formal appraisal, never show boredom or interrupt. If you find that you are talking more than the person being appraised, rethink your tactics. Use open questions—ones that demand more than a "Yes" or "No" answer—to find out what someone is thinking or feeling. The best questions often start with "What...?" because they make the fewest assumptions about the response, so try:

• What went well?
• What have we learned?

Identify activities and training that will develop the individual in their current role and prepare them for the future. Make clear the business case for any investment in development and training—does it help meet business, team, and individual objectives?

Take time to review the individual's achievements since the last appraisal and establish SMART objectives (see opposite) for the period until the next appraisal. Agree how and when you will measure change; there are many measurement tools at your disposal, including: observation; discussion during appraisals; informal one-to-one reviews; team meetings; examination of business results; other performance indicators; surveys; and assessment against competences.

Closing the appraisal

At the end of the appraisal, it is your turn as leader to ask for any feedback that might be helpful to your working relationship. Be sure to follow up on any support and training you have offered and review progress against agreed milestones. Throughout the year, examine how realistic the standards and deadlines were that you set at the appraisal.

Getting SMART—setting realistic objectives

SPECIFIC
Clearly expressed and within the control of the appraisee.

MEASURABLE
In terms of quantity, percentage, turnover, or some agreed qualitative measure.

AGREED
Between the two of you, rather than imposed.

REALISTIC
Challenging but achievable.

TIMELY
With schedules specified.

Learning from feedback

When you seek out and receive feedback, you develop your character as a leader. The two-way process of disclosing things about yourself and receiving comments on your performance builds trust. This in turn reduces the gap between your public and private faces and increases the authenticity of your leadership.

Seeking the truth

Once you have learned to both give and receive feedback skillfully and constructively, you will be ready to lead your team into greater self-awareness and higher levels of performance.

You can ask for feedback (formally or informally) from any of the people you come into contact with on a daily basis—members of your team, your superiors, clients, or suppliers.

The following series of questions is a good starting point for discussion with your appraiser, especially when you ask them to back up their answers with real examples:

• What do you see as my strengths?
• What do you think I am blind to?
• What development areas do you think I should be focusing on?
• What should I do less of/more of?
• What potential do you see in me?

Or, if you are using competences to set and monitor your targets, try the following phrasing:

• Which competences do I consistently demonstrate? (Enclose a copy of your competences.)
• Which competences do you think I could go on developing further?
• What changes do you foresee in the next 12 months and which competences do you think I should be focusing my development upon?

Becoming a rounded leader

A more formal means of gaining information about yourself—or any individual in your team—from a number of sources is 360° feedback. Ask a selection of 4–8 people at different levels in your organization to comment on the leadership behaviors they have observed you demonstrating over the last year. If appropriate, ask them to consider this against your stated competences. A questionnaire, set out like a customer satisfaction survey, will help give a consistent format for the replies.

IN FOCUS...
RUNNING 360° FEEDBACK

Ideally the 360° process should be managed by an objective external coach to ensure high-quality feedback, a balanced viewpoint, and anonymity for those individuals brave enough to feed back on their boss. However, if your organizational culture is open, and all agree to a no-blame approach, the review could be carried out internally.

When you receive feedback from others, compare it with your evaluation of yourself. Which leadership competences are your strengths? Which are your development areas? Which competences did you find most challenging last year and which will be even more demanding next year? Note the key development areas and think how you can broaden or deepen your knowledge, skills, or practice— for example reading up on a topic or attending a course. As well as providing valuable insight into others' perceptions of your leadership, 360° feedback is an invaluable tool for helping you prepare for your appraisal discussion with your manager or mentor.

Developing yourself

In this action-orientated world, many of us devote insufficient time and energy to our own development. Yet dedicated time for self-development is absolutely essential when it comes to growing your character and your own individual brand of leadership, as well as the attitudes, skills, and behaviors that will exemplify leadership to others.

TIP

LISTEN TO YOURSELF

Review your own progress by questioning yourself: are you building on your strengths and minimizing your weaknesses? Are you training your team and delegating to them successfully? Are you scheduling time to develop key relationships?

Reflecting and reviewing

The best way to accelerate your development and increase awareness of yourself and of others is through regular review and reflection. Put aside an hour every week for self-analysis and contemplation.

Start by reviewing your current development needs. Ask yourself how much of your activity the preceding week contributed to achieving your stated vision and objectives. Next, look at your future development needs and assess your progress against your stated leadership competences. Finally, consider the ideas you have for the next steps in your career; are you honing the skills now that you know will be needed for your career progress?

ASK YOURSELF... ABOUT YOUR DEVELOPMENT NEEDS

- Are your most time-consuming tasks related to processes? Do you need to develop time or project management skills, or planning abilities?
- Are your most time-consuming tasks related to content? Do you need to address a lack of knowledge in areas like marketing, finance, sales, or IT?
- Are your most time-consuming tasks related to people? Do you need training in recruitment, motivation, teambuilding, coaching, or delegating?

Journaling

Great leaders possess self-awareness and character—attributes acquired through reflection and self-analysis, but also through dealing regularly with real-life situations. Using a private journal to write down what you have learned about yourself in your day-to-day life can be very helpful. Record, for example, how you have helped someone else develop and learn, and how this has honed your own strengths as a leader.

Use your journal to make observations about how you respond to different conditions—what happens when you are tired or stressed? The pages of the journal can help you record and work through relationships that you are enjoying or struggling with, and to reflect on the highs and lows of your moods that you could not reveal in the workplace.

At first, journaling may seem like a chore; and initially your journal may not contain many connections or life-lessons. But after a number of weeks, you'll find that journaling becomes a habit that gives structure to your review and thinking time. Looking back over your journal will reveal how your leadership has developed, how you trust yourself, even in difficult situations, and what are the recurring issues.

TIP

KEEP YOUR FEET ON THE GROUND
Never become so grand that you lose touch with what it feels like to work with a customer on a project or to make a sale. Recognize that your role is now to help others enjoy this too.

IN FOCUS...
YOUR LONG-TERM DEVELOPMENT

As you mature as a leader, you will need to undertake weekly reviews of your development and achievements. However, you should also take time to think about your long-term goals, and your progress toward them. How well are you living up to your life principles? How have you dealt with disappointment and adversity? Have you managed to increase your level of performance? Have you fulfilled commitments to yourself and others? Are you happy in your career? What are your next steps? The more you learn, the more you realize you still have to learn. At this point, you might consider seeking advice from a career counsellor.

Balancing work and life

Most people would say that they want to be healthy, happy, and make a valued contribution at work to a successful organization. Creating and maintaining this sense of well-being is an integral part of your role as a leader. It involves taking a measured view of the balance between work and life and having realistic expectations of your team.

TIP

ACCENTUATE THE POSITIVE

Promote a healthy work–life balance and you'll not only avoid the pitfalls of stress and burnout in your team, but generate real benefits to the business. Happy staff deliver better results and empathetic customer service; staff retention and recruitment then become easier.

Attending to different needs

Good leaders know their team, their capabilities, and what motivates them. The real skill, though, is being able to use this knowledge to balance the needs of the task, the team, and the team members.

Maintaining this equilibrium is not always easy, because emphasis inevitably shifts from one area to another. For example, bursts of intense effort may be needed to meet tight deadlines—fine once in a while, but exhausting on a regular basis.

Similarly, the leader may sometimes have to focus on one member of the team who is not pulling their weight, or perhaps finding certain tasks difficult; but absolving them from obtaining agreed team standards for no obvious reason is clearly not acceptable.

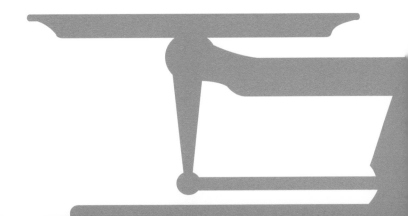

Managing stress

If you have built a strong team in good times, it will withstand short-term pressures, but you may need to invest time in team meetings and calm tensions to maintain balance. Your goal should be to keep your team members stretched but not stressed. Remember that stresses are cumulative: a team member may be able to tolerate stress at work for a short while if the other aspects of their life are running well.

✔ CHECKLIST ACHIEVING BALANCE IN YOUR LIFE

	YES	NO
• I often buy new books and have time to read them	☐	☐
• People remark on how open I am to new ideas	☐	☐
• I have a regular exercise routine	☐	☐
• I usually get a good night's sleep	☐	☐
• I have enough energy to see me through each day	☐	☐
• I express my feelings	☐	☐
• I know who I am and that's fine	☐	☐
• I have a clear sense of purpose in my life and make a real contribution at work	☐	☐
• I feel loved and able to give love to others	☐	☐

Inspiring and encouraging

From the way they formulate and express their overarching vision to the thought that they put into everyday interactions, which is the glue of any team relationship, you will find that leaders encourage and inspire others around them at every level of activity.

HOW TO... INSPIRE THROUGH YOUR VISION

State your vision in highly positive terms

⬇

Encourage others to enrich the vision by describing success in their own terms

⬇

Contextualize the vision—describe when, where, and with who it will be achieved

Setting a good example

One of the basic rules of leadership is that in order to inspire others you must aspire to be a model of excellence yourself. Of course, your personal journey toward excellence will never end, but it will give you two vital qualities—the desire to learn, and, in turn, that will lead to the humility of knowing how much more you have to learn.

You role is all about providing inspiration, and that starts with a clear vision for a better future, which you will need to communicate to your team on a daily basis through your words and actions:

• Make it clear to others that they have the capability and power to make a difference—that their unique attributes can help achieve the vision.

• Bring hope for the future to sustain people through change and adversity; if people feel overwhelmed and slow down, bring them back to the vision with simple messages that show the next small steps forward.

• Point out progress made and signs of success on the way to fill people once again with confidence and the desire to go forward.

• Praise new ideas and the courage demonstrated in new ventures.

• Keep team members stretched—one step ahead of what they thought they could do.

• Keep positive: explain that experiments that do not work are not failures—just feedback; turn setbacks into positive impetus for change.

Taking opportunities

Think how many opportunities you have in a single day to interact with your team, colleagues, bosses, and other stakeholders. Over 100 contacts a day—by phone, email, face-to-face, etc.—is not unusual for today's busy leaders and managers. Each of these interactions is an opportunity to encourage, inspire, and make your leadership felt.

When you make every meeting count, you create thousands of potential advocates for you, your team, your vision, and your organization. Moments add up to real commercial gain.

Focusing on the now

Inspiring people is less about delivering impassioned speeches and having a forceful personality, and more about focus and consistency. Treat everyone you deal with as a valued customer. Place them at the center of your universe for the duration of any interaction you have. Give them your full attention whether you are speaking face-to-face or on the phone. Be dependable in your daily interactions: your consistency builds trust and peace of mind in your team members, freeing them to focus on their key tasks rather than worrying about you.

BEING POSITIVE

FAST TRACK	OFF TRACK
Telling someone you enjoy working with them	Complaining to someone that you feel tired or ill
Smiling at people—sincerely, with your eyes	Being too shy to enjoy life or try new things
Thanking others for honest feedback	Excusing your falling standards
Controlling your emotions	Demotivating others just because you feel demotivated

TIP

ZAP, DON'T SAP
At every meeting, give people a zap —a quick burst of positive energy— and avoid the sap— anything that leaves them discouraged.

Chapter 3

Leading through challenges

In business, change is a constant. Organizations must constantly adapt to new realities and create opportunities for growth. It is your role as a leader to steer these changes, encourage others to take on new challenges, and project credibility and integrity even in times of uncertainty.

Focusing on the future

As a leader, you'll need to make tough decisions, plan a course of action, and take your team with you. The best way to achieve this is to involve your team from the start; explain what criteria your judgement is based upon and how plans are connected to other activities in the organization.

Making decisions

Leaders set the agenda in three key areas—by determining the direction in which the organization will move, by shaping how the organization does business, and by setting the pace of change. Any decisions you make in any of these three key areas should be based on objective criteria; for example, in a choice between two equally attractive options that require substantial investment, you should be able to explain why your decision was the best one in the circumstances.

Keeping objective

A weighted assessment will make clear the criteria you can use to make a decision and give your decision transparency. In the simple example below, a decision has to be made to adopt one of two projects—A or B; both seem attractive and have similar costs. To carry out the assessment, first engage with your team to make a list of criteria that the projects should satisfy. Not all criteria are of equal importance, so give each one a score from 1 to 10 depending on how valuable the team considers it to be. Check that the criteria are rounded—not all skewed toward finance, for example. Score each option (A and B) out of 10 on each criterion, and multiply each score by its corresponding weighting. Add the scores to see which project fulfils the criteria best.

WEIGHTED ASSESSMENT

CRITERIA	WEIGHTING	SCORE: PLAN A	SCORE: PLAN B	PLAN A x WEIGHTING	PLAN B x WEIGHTING
Maximize long-term customer satisfaction	10	6	9	60	90
Maximize return on investment	9	5	4	45	36
Maximize sustainability	8	9	4	72	32
Maximize high quality standards	8	6	10	48	80
Maximize long-term profit potential	8	8	5	64	40
Maximize staff satisfaction	7	2	10	14	70
Maximize added value for customers	7	6	8	42	56
Minimize hassle and administrative complexity	5	10	7	50	35
Maximize fun and interesting work	4	3	8	12	32
TOTAL				407	471

ASK YOURSELF...
WHAT'S OUR COMPETITIVE ADVANTAGE?

- What business are we not in?
- What are our core values?
- What business are we in?
- Do we differentiate ourselves by offering our customers unique benefits?
- Do we differentiate ourselves by offering our customers better prices?

TIP

OPEN CHANNELS

Keep listening to everyone you are connected to; share ideas, and keep open channels of communication that are needed now and may be needed in the future.

Locating change

Deciding which opportunities to explore, exploit, and reject requires a crystal clear understanding of your organization's purpose and mission. In particular, you must understand what gives your business its edge over the competition and use this knowledge to guide your future focus. Competitive advantage is based on what customers value and the organization's strengths relative to the competition. It takes into account external trends that will help or hinder momentum in the chosen direction.

Setting the pace

When orchestrating strategic change within an organization, you need to give careful consideration to timing. If the rate of change is too slow, the process may simply run out of momentum; if it is too fast, you risk creating stress and burnout.

Aim for a sustainably fast pace at which your major initiatives will have started to produce measurable results within a year—even if the whole process is scheduled to take much longer.

Steering significant organizational change is hard work: typically, there is a trough in visible results just at the point where you need the most effort and commitment from all stakeholders. Investors, in particular, may lose heart in this trough period, so need to be reminded regularly of the benefits to come. Plan in "quick wins" throughout the process—achievements that have high visibility but require little effort. Celebrate and publicize these successes, and drip-feed messages about how project milestones and results achieved so far are bringing the vision nearer to reality.

Integrating change

Everything in an organization is connected. Processes and systems in one area impact on others. As a leader, you should make explicit the connections between different plans and explain how each one contributes to the vision. Understanding the bigger picture will help your team to recognize their role and commit to change. The message can be a complex one, so communicate little and often, and check regularly how well people have understood the connections between plans, departments, and roles.

Connected organizational plans

Human Resources and Organization Development Plan

Operations Plan (products and services)

Marketing Plan

Strategic Business Plan

Finance, IT Sourcing, and R & D Plans

Enabling change

Opportunities for innovation exist at every level of an organization, and leaders must continuously plan change to move forward and stay ahead of competitors. Processes, systems, skills, and competences can always be improved, or the whole business can be moved in an entirely new direction. Leading change requires a sense of balance between priorities and keen awareness of responses among all stakeholders.

EXPECT DISSENT

When you introduce high-level change, expect at least 50 percent of your people to hate the idea.

Balancing priorities

A key leadership skill is keeping a balance between short-term improvement and long-term innovation. If you are continuously improving at the margins while neglecting strategic innovation, it will lead to organizational myopia and the risk of missing out on the next big trend. Conversely, constant innovation at the core can be counterproductive because people will eventually feel worn out and unwilling to take on yet another new initiative.

Maintaining stability

The leader seeks to progress with both short- and long-term change while maintaining equilibrium. This can be a challenge: while most people will quickly accommodate small steps that visibly improve the way things are done, bold strategic innovation requires the leader to inspire people, sometimes for many years, before seeing a return. Before implementing change, discuss its implications with multiple small groups of stakeholders. People should feel free to ask questions and express their concerns. Help people to see what will remain the same—these things can provide an anchor of stability for those who dislike change.

Reacting to change

People react differently to change. At one extreme are the innovators who may be so eager to walk toward a new future that they do not realize that no one has followed them. At the other end are the stragglers, who join in only when everyone else has moved on. Traditionalists hang on to the past, viewing change as a threat. Surprisingly, they have one thing in common with the innovators—they respond with emotion to the impending change. The remainder—the cautious majority—are likely to weigh up the arguments put across on the basis of reason. As leader, you need to use both logic and emotion when explaining your plans. Be persistent and emphasize to everyone the benefits to come when the changes have been made.

  People take different lengths of time to adjust to change and you should prepare for the long haul: typically, the adjustment process falls into distinct phases, which are characterized by different sets of behaviors. Be aware that people who adopt change quickly can show impatience with the slowest; this can lead to conflict within the team, which you may be called upon to help resolve.

HOW TO...
RECOGNIZE THE STAGES OF ADAPTATION TO CHANGE

Expectation: anticipation, excitement

Standstill: numbness, disorientation, denial

Lack of energy: missing "the old days"

Conflict in the team: resistance, anger, squabbling

Incompetence: depression, apathy, resentment

Low output: feelings of loss, the need to let go, detachment from others

Working longer hours: gradual acceptance of the new reality

Problem solving: exploring the new, experimenting, hope

Increased effectiveness: search for new purpose, commitment to new situation

Productivity: re-engagement, commitment, motivation

Energizing the team

When you put together a group of people—anywhere between two and several thousand—you won't automatically get a team. For a group to become a team, it must be energized and focused and it must think of success as a collective rather than individual aim. Carrying out this transformation is your job as a leader.

TIP

BE INCLUSIVE
Welcome newcomers to the team and encourage them to speak at meetings and engage with the group from an early stage. Don't allow new recruits to become accustomed to a backseat role.

Choosing your team

Selecting team members who will work together well, motivating the group, and dealing with conflict are the essential aspects of team leadership. And as increasing amounts of work are project-based, you need to develop team cohesion and focus quickly despite rapid changes in the mix of the team.

Invest time at the start of a project to choose or strengthen the team; your investment will be repaid later in the project cycle when the group comes under pressure. Select team members with complementary skills and talents that come into play at different stages of a project. As a minimum, your team should have a good mix of the following thinking styles:

• **The leader**—ensures everyone understands the objectives; motivates and communicates.
• **The creative**—an imaginative thinker who has bold concepts at the outset of a project and provides ideas when the team is stuck.
• **The analyst**—the problem-solver who tests the plan at every stage.
• **The facilitator**—has good interpersonal skills, is sensitive to the group dynamic, and acts as the "glue" in a team.
• **The administrator**—pays attention to details and keeps the team on time and focused on the task. If the team is small, members may need to be able to fill more than one of the above roles.

Running your team

Make clear the roles that each individual will play in the team. Devolve decision-making to the group as far as possible, and encourage everyone to participate in decisions—this will help to spread the ownership of goals. Set out shared values, develop ground rules that describe how the team will work together from the start, and watch the way that group dynamics develop; take action immediately at the first sign of conflict or if an individual starts to act in a way not consistent with the agreed team rules. Be supportive, give credit for good cooperative work and knowledge shared, and always celebrate team achievements.

When you build and manage your team successfully, group members will start to make one another accountable for achieving individual tasks, and begin to appreciate and share in collective success. Trust will build as each member commits to actions at team meetings and carries them out as promised.

The signs of an energized team

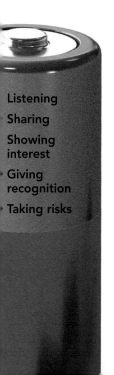

- Listening
- Sharing
- Showing interest
- Giving recognition
- Taking risks

- Being trusting, honest, and open
- Collaborating
- Innovating
- Supporting one another

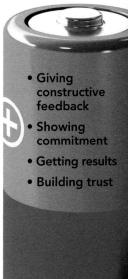

- Giving constructive feedback
- Showing commitment
- Getting results
- Building trust

Leading difficult people

Building a successful team depends on cooperation between all members of the group. But what if an individual just won't play ball? Unproductive confrontations with you as leader or between team members can take up a lot of your time, create a bad atmosphere, and stop you achieving your aims, so finding positive ways to deal with disagreement or difficult individuals is a key leadership skill.

TIP

GET ADVANCE WARNINGS

Get to know your team members really well. You'll be able to notice changes in their mood, patterns of work, or work–life balance, which often signal stress.

Dealing with conflict

Conflict arises when two people stop listening to each other and approach a situation from their own point of view. When you are involved in this situation, it is hard to be objective and remind yourself that people are rarely awkward "on purpose"—generally they are doing their best in a situation that they find hard. As leader, you must look beyond the immediate confrontation to try and understand what it is really happening and discover the roots of the hostility.

The first place to start is with yourself—your position means you may be an important factor in a team member's dissatisfaction. Individual differences in outlook, behavior, and style can generate tension—which can be used constructively to stimulate creativity and enrich the perspective of the team or, if left unmanaged, can cause division.

ASK YOURSELF... IS IT ME?

- Have I explained new initiatives clearly—could they be causing insecurity or anxiety?
- Do I come across as approachable and accessible?
- Have I made unreasonable demands?
- Have I been fair in my praise or my criticism?
- Am I portraying the right image for a leader?

WHY PEOPLE BECOME DIFFICULT

CAUSE	EFFECT	REMEDY
Reaching the limits of current capability	Team member makes errors and cannot do the job to the required standard. Other team members become impatient.	Offer support and training over a reasonable timescale. If there is little improvement, their future in your team is limited.
Becoming disengaged	Rejection of the job; withdrawal from involvement with the team. Often caused by frustration when high achievers have been held back over time. Will have an adverse effect on entire team.	Explore causes in a one-to-one discussion. If you have inherited this individual, you need to release the burden of all the past broken promises and build new trust. Consider counselling.
Getting distracted	Focus moves elsewhere reducing effectiveness. The cause is often personal and while colleagues will sympathize initially, they will soon tire of the issue.	Listen sympathetically and arrange time off if you think this will help to solve the problem. Make sure that you recognize when the problem goes beyond your ability and ask for further help.
Losing motivation	Too little or too much delegation or challenge in the role can bring about demotivation and decreased effectiveness. The individual can quickly have a negative effect on team morale.	Get to know what particularly motivates each member of the team. Ask yourself if you are over- or under-delegating to the person. Over-delegation can cause paralyzing fear of failure.

Meeting standards

It is tempting to work around a "difficult" person, but doing so undermines the standards you have set for your team and your own position as leader. Other members of the team will soon realize that being difficult means you can avoid tasks you dislike. As their leader, you should explore all courses of action to bring about improvement in a reasonable timescale. Bear in mind that many people do not cope well in an adversarial situation and may even sabotage their own future because they cannot see a way out of the conflict. If fair and open discussion, and your support, fails to achieve necessary changes, you will need to work within your organization's disciplinary policy and procedures to deal with the "difficult" person, to prevent their adverse effect on the rest of the team from escalating and causing further, wider problems.

Balancing targets

Results are what it's all about. They are the synthesis of all your thinking, planning, and enabling as a leader. To get what you want from a project, you should clarify standards and objectives from the outset. Your targets need to be realistic, and they also require a means of measuring the performance of all involved.

Getting the right results

The targets you set for your team should stretch everyone but also be realistic, in line with the SMART criteria. Ensure that the aims you set are balanced; alongside financial targets, include goals in areas such as speed of response, product and service quality, customer and team satisfaction, and brand development. List the desired results in each of four key areas—customers, operations, people, and finance—so that no one objective takes assumed priority over another. Review results in each area monthly so that you can prove progress to yourself, your team, and your investors.

FINANCE
- Profits
- Investment
- Sales
- Cash

Setting service-level agreements

Clarify the results you expect from interactions between purchasers and providers or between departments in a service level agreement. You can then present the obligations in a written format—minimum or maximum standards and timescales, or other measures of reliability or availability, for example:
- **Our obligations:** to provide you with information within four hours of request, etc.
- **Your obligations:** to respond to service requests within four hours of phone call enquiry, etc.

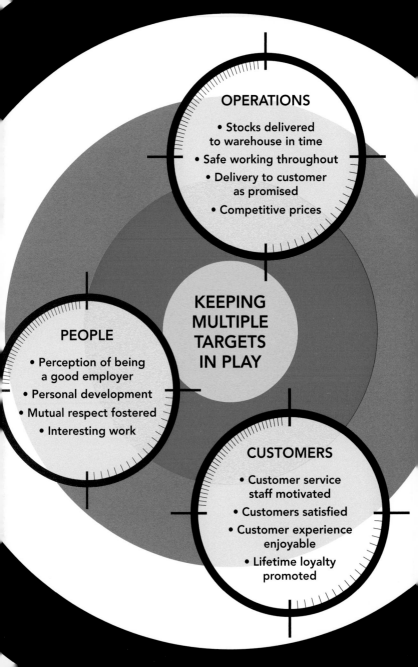

OPERATIONS
- Stocks delivered to warehouse in time
- Safe working throughout
- Delivery to customer as promised
- Competitive prices

KEEPING MULTIPLE TARGETS IN PLAY

PEOPLE
- Perception of being a good employer
- Personal development
- Mutual respect fostered
- Interesting work

CUSTOMERS
- Customer service staff motivated
- Customers satisfied
- Customer experience enjoyable
- Lifetime loyalty promoted

Improving confidence

Confidence is a cornerstone of good leadership. Especially in times of uncertainty, upheaval, or crisis, believing in yourself and making the right decisions will give you credibility and integrity, which in turn will enhance the organization's reputation and build trust in all stakeholders.

Being prepared

Confidence can come in a number of different ways. It comes from experience as your track record as a leader improves. It comes from having well-formed plans and anticipating challenges, and it comes from the knowledge that you have a strong business built on productive working relationships.

TIP

BOOST YOURSELF
Regularly affirm your own strengths as a leader by privately listing your abilities and achievements. This will give you an instant confidence boost and banish that internal critic living in your head.

Communicating with confidence

While there are no shortcuts to building confidence, there are ways that you can project confidence to your team and to your stakeholders.
• Use confident language to describe your vision. Listen and learn from political leaders, who characteristically employ optimistic language that suggests a future state—words such as "innovative," "special," "original," "latest," "breakthrough," "updated," and "leading-edge." Used regularly, this kind of vocabulary spreads through the organization.
• Deliver your vision messages in sound bites no more than 30 seconds long that sum up the benefits of the opportunities you wish to explore.
• Consider giving your new vision a badge—a look or a logo to symbolize the change you want to happen. By implication, those who use the new language or adopt the new symbols share the leader's vision and have committed to the change.

Acknowledging ideas

Your inner confidence will grow when you behave in a confident manner and gain the trust of your team and colleagues. Ability and willingness to devolve power and decision-making is one characteristic that marks out a confident leader, so take every opportunity to involve others and empower them to act on their ideas. Be open about what is not working for you, your customers, suppliers, or employees; your frankness will be interpreted as an expression of confidence because you approach success and adversity with equal zeal. Encourage people to discover and understand situations for themselves rather than spoon-feeding them issues and answers—remember your power increases as you give it away.

FACE YOUR FEARS

Confidence comes from self-knowledge; understanding your thoughts and actions gives you the ability to control them. A good way to become more self-assured is to face your fears—do that presentation, confront your difficult CEO, and reply to that demanding client—now!

Being consistent

As a leader, your every word and action is scrutinized by your team and could be given far more significance than you intended. Perceptions of you as a confident leader can be undermined by conscious or unconscious slips, so try and think in a measured way about the kind of signals you are sending out. Consistency and calmness in adversity are characteristics that most people will perceive as confidence.

CHECKLIST STAYING CALM IN ADVERSITY

	YES	NO
• Do I know what triggers an emotional overreaction in me?	☐	☐
• Can I spot the signs of stress in myself?	☐	☐
• Am I able to delay my response for a few seconds before I respond?	☐	☐

Creating networks

As a leader, you will need to create, develop, and maintain networks of contacts within and far beyond your own organization. Networks enable you to exchange information with others, share resources, gain referrals, leads, or recommendations, test ideas, build long-term relationships, and help others in return.

Reaping the rewards

TIP

MAKE ADVOCATES
Distinguish between associates, allies, and advocates in your network. Associates are those within your sphere of influence; allies are those who will recommend you to others if prompted; while advocates will actively promote you without being asked.

Networks are your eyes and ears. They warn you about trends and developments in markets, signal opportunities and threats, and help identify niches for you to exploit. So, the wider your network, the more responsive you will be to market changes.

Your network is also a huge learning circle, where you can tap into valuable lessons and experience, gain some different perspectives on new initiatives, and get grounded in reality by your colleagues. Networks put you in touch with suppliers, customers, partners, and financiers, and may help your negotiations with useful information from others' relationships with these third parties.

Building effective networks can take a few months or a few years; maintaining them takes a lifetime. To be a successful networker, you must accept that it is a two-way process in that the more you give to others, the more you gain. People will quickly categorize you as a "taker" if you only get in touch when you want something.

TAG YOURSELF

Wear a large-print name tag to all networking events. Position the tag high on your right lapel or shoulder, so that it can be easily read when someone shakes hands with you. For a good conversation opener, add an interesting tag to your name, for example, John Smith, Marketing Wizard.

Attending events

Professional bodies and business associations often run events specifically to provide opportunities for networking; however, any chance to meet with colleagues, clients, and suppliers is a *de facto* networking event. Aim to attend two or three such events a month, and at each, try to talk in-depth with two or three people with potential to help you rather than scattering your business cards to as many people as possible in a crowded room. Ideally, you should leave each conversation with a sense of mutual commitment. Always follow up the same or the next day with any information or contact promised.

HOW TO... BUILD AN EFFECTIVE NETWORK

List all potentially useful contacts and ask your team to do the same

↓

Include former workplaces and colleagues and personal contacts of family and friends

↓

Review your list sector by sector to remind yourself of people

↓

Think creatively about what you can offer to help your network contacts in return

↓

Keep in touch regularly and always follow up on promises

NETWORKING IN PERSON

FAST TRACK

OFF TRACK

FAST TRACK	OFF TRACK
Having your business cards ready	Forgetting to study the guest list
Preparing some introductory questions or icebreakers	Not researching the people you would like to meet
Introducing yourself clearly, briefly, and memorably	Mismatching what you say with your body language
Leaving a physical gap in your group that invites someone to join	Barging into groups with no eye contact first

Learning from entrepreneurs

Entrepreneurs enjoy creating value by taking advantage of opportunities and solving problems for customers. Leaders in organizations of all sizes—and all ages—can learn from their bold approach, it is just a question of looking in new ways at old problems and producing innovative solutions.

Finding opportunities

What marks out entrepreneurs is their preparedness to listen to their customers, see new opportunities, and back their ideas with drive and determination. They also have a refreshing attitude to "failure"—everything is viewed as a useful experience, and trial and error is seen as a legitimate path to success. Entrepreneurs think ahead, don't accept the status quo, and ask questions that begin with "Why?", "Why not?", and "What if...?".

Large corporations are increasingly encouraging their leaders to show entrepreneurial zeal within the mature organization—a phenomenon called intrapreneurship.

Looking at your business with an entrepreneurial mindset will help you generate ideas for maximizing opportunities for growth that no one else has seen—either within or outside the organization.

Develop your own entrepreneurial leadership skills by asking more questions of customers and colleagues—what issues cause you regular hassle? How can we help you? Celebrate both successes and failures as signs of entrepreneurship, and be sure to reward the contributions people make to creating value for the business, and responding flexibly to opportunities to solve problems for customers. Scrutinize your business for new opportunities. Think hard, and above all, think creatively.

TIP

HARNESS TALENT
You may have a natural entrepreneur already in your team. Give them the space to innovate and put up with their often challenging nature and you will gain a real asset.

UNDERUTILIZED INFORMATION OR ASSETS

Can we sell our information externally?

Can we get better performance by outsourcing?

Can we lease our assets?

WAYS TO CHANGE THE BUSINESS MODEL

Will acquisitions boost our capabilities?

Can we cut out the middleman?

Should we support employee spin-offs?

Where to look for entrepreneurial ideas

NEW MARKETS, NEW CUSTOMERS

Can we change our pricing structures?

Can we do what we do for our best customers for others?

How do we extend our markets?

NEW PRODUCTS AND SERVICES

Can we sell our products or services as a system?

Can we turn internal services into sales?

Can we meet unmet needs?

Chapter 4
Developing leaders

Leaders know all about the importance of realizing visions. They understand that any vision must have the organization's future at heart. By discovering and developing up-and-coming leadership talent, today's leaders play a vital role in the future of organizations across the world. When they get it right, their legacy will live on in generations of future leaders.

Investing in the future

For an organization to expand, it needs to invest in the development of the new leaders that will take it forward. Individuals who display leadership potential should be considered as an important asset that will grow if nurtured, and will be lost if not.

Appointing talent

A successful organization needs a ready supply of new leaders. Recruiting all future leaders from outside of your organization simply isn't cost effective; it takes a substantial amount of management time and money to find the right candidates and bring them up to speed. By contrast, leaders who are promoted from within your organization already have a very good understanding of your organization's culture and working methods, and will have been nurtured and trained by you to have exactly the suite of skills and knowledge required to take on their new role.

Realizing potential

One of your key goals as a leader is to recognize leadership qualities in others, and to know how to encourage and assist future leaders so they can realize their full potential. It can be helpful to think of leadership growing in a series of transitions in self-awareness, skill, and responsibility. Recognizing these crucial changes in others, and responding appropriately to them, will help to accelerate the development of new leaders.

Each stage on the path to leadership will bring different challenges—not only in taking on new attitudes and responsibilities, but also leaving behind familiar and comfortable behaviors. This can be a highly stressful time for newly appointed leaders and the individual may not recognize or expect the strains and associated emotions of transition.

Feelings of uncertainty, being overwhelmed, and loss of confidence can immobilize new leaders at the very point that they are expected to shine. Moreover, it is unlikely that the person making the transition will feel comfortable raising these concerns with you, their manager, for fear of appearing to fail.

SPOT THE SIGNS OF CHANGE

Train yourself as a leader to recognize the signs of transition between different stages of leadership, and be ready to support individuals as they push for the next level.

✔ # CHECKLIST **CREATING FUTURE LEADERS IN YOUR ORGANIZATION**

	YES	NO
• Do you look for win–win situations for you/your team/ other teams/the organization?	☐	☐
• Do you demonstrate good stewardship of talent for the whole organization's benefit?	☐	☐
• Do you have a track record of unselfishly releasing potential leaders to take up development opportunities?	☐	☐
• Do you initiate the development of potential leaders?	☐	☐
• Do you encourage members of your team to apply for internal promotion or transfers?	☐	☐

LEARN FROM MISTAKES

Making mistakes is a natural part of the learning process. When you guide one of your team through the different stages of leadership, turn their errors into learning points.

Recognizing leadership stages

The first sign of leadership potential is a transition from being self-focused, and simply performing to a high standard in your own role, to becoming more aware of, and helpful to, others. Potential leaders then start taking on more responsibility and begin questioning the ways things are done and coming up with ideas for doing things differently.

As the potential leader develops, others in the organization start to recognize their vision and that they have a talent for spotting opportunities that will benefit the team or the organization as a whole. They thrive on added responsibility, and when they have a team to manage, they contribute at a higher level, work well with peers, and show a talent for developing team members. Others naturally gravitate toward them to sound out ideas; this may be formalized into mentoring or coaching roles. Ultimately, they start to develop the skills needed to nurture the next generation of leaders in your organization.

HOW TO...
HELP POTENTIAL LEADERS MAKE TRANSITIONS

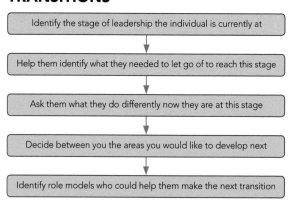

Identify the stage of leadership the individual is currently at

Help them identify what they needed to let go of to reach this stage

Ask them what they do differently now they are at this stage

Decide between you the areas you would like to develop next

Identify role models who could help them make the next transition

MAKING LEADERSHIP TRANSITIONS

STAGE OF LEADERSHIP	TAKING UP THE NEW	LETTING GO OF THE OLD
Self-awareness	• Doing more than the job description • Performing excellently • Accepting more responsibility • Inheriting corporate memory • Becoming a team player • Suggesting improvements	• Doing the job description • Keeping yourself to yourself • Focusing on your own performance • Carrying out everything to the letter • Referring to "I"
Other-awareness	• Greater empathy • Helping fellow workers • Being diplomatic • Looking for win–win solutions • Preferring people to procedures • Referring to "We"	• Conforming to previous procedures • Carrying out without challenging • Not questioning the brief • Going your own way • Focusing only on own excellence
Responsibility	• Looking for added value opportunities • Accepting responsibility for growth and results • Understanding vision and purpose, and communicating commitment to them • Prioritizing high value opportunities • Making difficult choices	• Valuing people based only on technical or professional excellence • Using only financial indicators • Focusing on people not results • Going for the easy option • Achieving what is asked • Blaming everyone else for poor performance
Development	• Developing talent for the benefit of all • Helping others to perform well • Becoming a mentor • Planning development opportunities • Choosing a team to complement you • Nurturing future leaders	• Prioritizing results above people • Holding on to good people • Failing to delegate enough • Allowing too little time with others • Postponing training if under pressure • Underestimating time for meetings
Embodiment	• Facilitating others to grow • Initiating peer networks • Acting as a leader of leaders • Mentoring/coaching leaders	• Focusing only on the organization • Sacrificing social life • Allowing leader-centric power games

Coaching for success

A good coach can accelerate the development of your future leaders, helping them to manage the transitions they need to make to gain leadership experience and develop the suite of competences required to be a top leader within your organization.

TIP

VISUALIZE LEADERSHIP

Encourage those you are coaching to develop a detailed mental image of themselves as an effective leader, and to use this vision to motivate and commit themselves to making changes.

Releasing potential

It isn't easy to find time to invest in coaching your potential leaders, but there is a considerable return to you, your team, and the organization, if you do. The selection of coaches needs to be undertaken with care—the careers of some of the brightest prospects in your organization will be in their hands. You may choose to coach your potential leaders yourself, or you may prefer to appoint other internal or external coaches. Whoever you choose, they must have the right business and coaching experience or have received training on how to coach effectively.

Challenging and supporting

The hallmark of a skilled coach is knowing when to challenge and when to support the individual being coached. Successful coaches work to build self-awareness and release potential, by, for example, unblocking limiting or constricting beliefs or confronting unhelpful behaviors. They encourage those they are coaching to reflect, think strategically, release creativity, and feel good about who they are.

The results of successful coaching should be an increased self-appreciation in your future leaders of their personal strengths, competences, approach, and actions. These, in turn, should align with your organization's values and aims.

- **What do you want to achieve?**
- **What is the current situation?**
- **What similar project have you completed in the past?**
- **What problems might occur?**
- **How could you overcome problems?**

GOOD OPEN COACHING QUESTIONS

- **When could that be done?**
- **What help might you need?**
- **What can you do?**
- **What experiences and skills do you have that would be helpful?**
- **Who else could help with this?**

Structuring sessions

Effective coaching needs to be structured, so set up a series of one-on-one coaching sessions for each of your potential leaders.

Use the coaching sessions to find out where the individual is now in their development as a leader, and where they aim to be. Encourage them to set goals and explore options to reach them. Identify any obstacles that may make success difficult, and offer support. Throughout the coaching process, be sure to keep your questions open, so that they demand more than a "yes" or "no" answer—this encourages the individual to think everything through fully. At the end of each session, ask the individual to draw up an action plan based on your discussion, clearly setting out the goals to be achieved, the activities needed to reach these goals, the resources required, a realistic timetable for achieving the goals, and the outcomes expected. These should be reassessed and the success of the individual evaluated at subsequent sessions.

TIP

MAP OUT THE PROCESS

When providing coaching, explain what the process is, how long it will take, and what will be covered. Encourage the coachee to journal their progress.

Understanding the practicalities

The first step in a coaching program might be to set up a series of six sessions with each coachee over a period of 4–6 months: each session is likely to take 1–2 hours. The coach and coachee define a "contract" based on the needs and expectations of the coachee, and identify links to be made to the organization's Performance Review. Coaches usually leave the longest possible sustainable gap between sessions, to enable action in the workplace by the individual following each coaching session. Most coaching takes place face-to-face but individuals can be coached by email or telephone. Within bounds of confidentiality, coachees should be encouraged to give feedback to the organization because it is sponsoring the coaching; if the investment is to continue, individuals should be able to demonstrate through presentations, meetings, and on a practical level, business results, the effectiveness of their coaching.

Benefiting the business

Coaching and mentoring—especially of first line and middle managers—is often focused on specific issues or to help people make particular leadership transitions. In this case, experienced mentors from your organization may be most suitable. Senior managers may benefit from an external coach with more experience at board level. With successful coaching you may find leaders become better at innovating and developing the overall capability of their teams. The effects of coaching work through the organization and provide significant business benefits including:
• Retention of key executives
• Enhanced working relationships
• Greater alignment of individual/corporate objectives
• New perspectives on business issues.

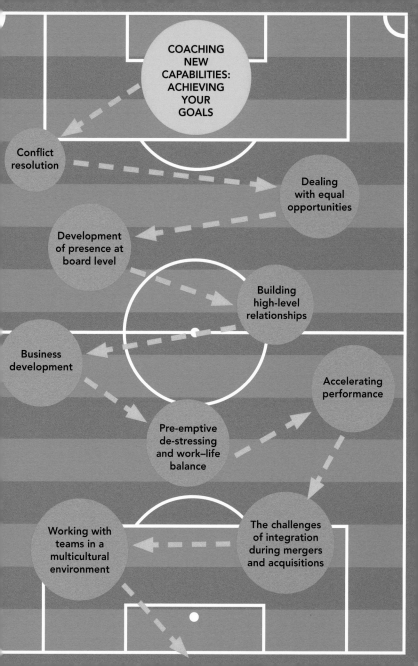

Adopting new leadership patterns

The 20th-century idea of a job for life is rapidly being superseded by the concept of the portfolio career. Today's leaders need to be skilled in change management because their own careers are almost certain to be characterized by frequent transition. The emphasis has shifted from excelling in a particular corporate position to excelling in one vital project—leading your own life based on consistent principles.

Profiting from change

In business today, leaders need to manage and inspire not just their core teams but groups of freelancers, temporary staff, and outsourcers. Engaging such potentially disparate groups to align them with the vision and values of the organization is the new leadership challenge. Leaders today may be heading up a virtual team—with members based globally—formed around a customer problem that needs solving or an innovative idea rather than a group of people physically working together for the same employer. Leaders with the ability to be agile, to build virtual networks, teams, and alliances quickly, will be the long-term winners.

In the coming years, leaders will look less and less to their employers to provide a framework or support system for their life—they will need to develop it themselves. As an individual aiming to survive in this rapidly changing environment, you will need to be excellent at understanding customer needs and have supreme confidence in your ability to deliver, and market, yourself. Thinking creatively and with vision, both about your career and personal mission, should become a life-long process and a central theme in your continued success.

Branding yourself

So how exactly do you develop yourself as a leader for the 21st century? One way of answering this question is to think of what you can deliver to your customers as a brand. Your brand signals your professional, technical, and functional knowledge and skills, and also your position in the market. Aim to develop yourself much as you would steer a brand. Shape your product (what you offer) to anticipate customer demand, and develop your identity to make the best fit with desirable clients. For example, should your next client be a small enterprise where you can work closely on your entrepreneurial acumen, or should it be a large corporation where you can refresh process management knowledge based on the latest research? Consider your next steps carefully; how they will shape your brand?

HOW TO...
DEVELOP
CONTINUOUSLY

Assess your competences and match with customer needs

↓

Take an assignment to stretch you

↓

Listen to customers; engage with others; join networks; initiate alliances

↓

Learn from best practice

↓

Recognize your potential for development

↓

Practice new skills and behaviors

↓

Refine your brand

↓

Identify your next direction for development

Index

Acknowledgments

Author's acknowledgments
Writing a book for Dorling Kindersley immediately involves you in teamwork at its best – a combination of many talents, much patience, and great commitment. I would like to thank Adèle Hayward and Peter Jones for their vision and stewardship throughout and Marek Walisiewicz for his inspiring leadership in bringing about the meld of visual impact and words, with his team of editors and designers, which has made this such an interesting project.

Publisher's acknowledgments
The publisher would like to thank Professor Naresh Pandit, Tom Albrighton, Neil Mason, Sarah Tomley, Hilary Bird for indexing, and Charles Wills for co-ordinating Americanization.

Picture credits
The publisher would like to thank the following for their kind permission to reproduce their photographs:
1 Getty Images: Steven Hunt; 4–5 Getty Images: David Madison; 9 iStockphoto.com: Dan Tero; 11 iStockphoto.com: Janne Ahvo; 12–13 iStockphoto.com: Ryan Burke; 14–15 iStockphoto.com: Sven Hoppe; 19 iStockphoto.com: Russell Tate; 23 iStockphoto.com: MistikaS; 26 Alamy Images: Barry Lewis; 29 iStockphoto.com: Shawn Gearhart; 34–35 iStockphoto.com: Andrey Prokhorov; 38–39 iStockphoto.com: Tim Inman; 48–49 iStockphoto.com: Lev Mel; 58–59 Alamy Images: Wasabi; 65 iStockphoto.com: Mark Murphy; 69 iStockphoto.com: Dean Turner.

Every effort has been made to trace the copyright holders. The publisher apologizes for any unintentional omission and would be pleased, in such cases, to place an acknowledgment in future editions of this book.